LINENS AND LACE

TRICIA FOLEY

TEXT BY
CLAIRE WHITCOMB

PHOTOGRAPHS BY
LILO RAYMOND

DESIGN BY
HENRIETTA CONDAK

CLARKSON POTTER/PUBLISHERS

Text copyright © 1990 by Tricia Foley
Photographs copyright © 1990 by Lilo Raymond

Published by Clarkson N. Potter, Inc., 201 East 50th Street, New York, New York
10022.

CLARKSON N. POTTER, POTTER, and colophon are trademarks of Clarkson N.
Potter, Inc.

Manufactured in Japan

Library of Congress Cataloging-in-Publication Data
Foley, Tricia.
    Linens and lace/Tricia Foley: photographs by Lilo Raymond: text by Claire
Whitcomb.— 1st ed.
        p.   cm.
    Includes bibliographical references
    1. Textile fabrics in interior decoration.   2. Linen.   3. Lace
making.   I. Whitcomb, Claire.   II. Title.
    TX315.F65   1990
    845'.046—dc20   90-34685
                                                                                      CIP

ISBN 0-517-57680-5
10 9 8 7 6 5 4 3 2 1
First Edition

ACKNOWLEDGMENTS

o those whose help and support made *Linens and Lace* a reality, I would like to extend my thanks.

To Lilo Raymond, whose work I've admired for years, for being a part of this project; to Claire Whitcomb, for her writing and contributions in navigating us through the hedges and over the moors in England in search of the history of lace; to Henrietta Condak for her beautiful design; and to Ellen Ivens for all her patience in tracking down our many resources.

To Lauren Shakely for her enthusiasm and guidance in the development of our book, to Nancy Novogrod for getting me started, and also to Isolde Motley, Howard Klein, and Carol Southern.

To my agents, Deborah Geltman and Gayle Benderoff, for always being there for me. To Colleen Heather Rogan, who was always eager and willing to help.

To my family, especially my mother, for her continuing support and to Nancy Lindemeyer for her understanding during this project.

To all my friends who shared their linens collections and opened their homes to us, especially Bill Steele and Matthew Mattiello, Susan Becher and Bruce Gilbert, Ellen and Bridget O'Neill, Margaret Ahern, and my friends at the Yaphank Historical Society for providing such a wonderful location for us.

To Gillian Moss at the Cooper-Hewitt Museum, New York, and to Laura Fisher, Bryce Revelly, and Elaine Wilmarth for sharing their years of experience with us.

And finally, to our friends in England who made us so welcome: Stephen Lunn, Dr. John Yallup, and Pat Perryman.

Thank you!

T.F.

CONTENTS

PREFACE

hen visiting antiques shops over the years I have always been drawn to the corners where trunks and cupboards are filled to brimming with white linens and where old baskets overflow with bits and pieces of lace and ribbons. I love searching through stacks of lace and linens, touching each item and turning it over until I come across the perfect find—something totally unexpected and, from that moment, impossible to live without.

Not only do the fabrics themselves appeal to me—the natural fibers of cotton and linen, the delicate intricacies of lace—but I am also drawn to the stories behind them. Who stitched, embroidered, tatted, and crocheted these beautiful pieces with such care? Each monogrammed hand towel, each lacy pillow sham has its own story.

Most of the linens and lace available at shops, estate sales, and even flea markets are "vintage linens," white and ecru linens and laces made from about the mid-19th century through the 1930s. Surviving pieces from before that time are usually of museum quality, and are true heirlooms; these pieces should be treated with respect.

For everyday pleasure, vintage linens are more practical; the collector attracted to the individuality of handmade pieces will find the related arts of embroidery, crochet, filet, and knitted lace truly satisfying.

Those who wish to collect linens and lace for purely practical, rather than antiquarian, reasons, should also consider contemporary products. The resurgence of interest in the romantic appeal of antique and vintage linens has led boutiques, department stores, and mail-order catalogues to offer a wealth of well-made contemporary linens and reproductions of classic lace designs. It is even possible to find contemporary handmade lace—though this is rare and expensive.

Whether your interest is in the history, the decorative versatility, or just the sensual appeal of linens and lace, I hope you will find inspiration in these pages. My cousin once said that handmade lace is like snowflakes—no two patterns are the same. Likewise each collector has special personal reasons for falling in love with linens and lace.

INTRODUCTION

he story of linens and lace in the home is a romantic one. It begins in the bedroom, where aristocratic ladies dressed their beds and vanities just as they would themselves—with fabrics that pleased both the eye and the senses. From the bedchambers of royalty, linens and lace have moved into other rooms and other types of homes to bring welcome luxury into the lives of many.

Interestingly, although linen has had a long decorating history, lace has made only a relatively recent appearance in the home. The Romans and the Egyptians surely slept on linens as finely woven as those used by the 16th-century Venetians, but only the latter embellished their bedrooms with the fabric we now call lace.

In the 1540s Venetian embroiderers began trying to improve on the fine weave of linen with cutwork. After cutting away bits of a fabric's warp and weft, they stitched the remaining web of threads into intricate, lacy motifs. Soon these needlewomen realized that even more wondrous patterns could be created if they left linen behind and relied strictly on *punto in aria*—literally "stitches in air," or needle lace. Their technique for making this free-form lace is illustrated by the legend of a knight who presented a lady with a rose when he went off to the

Crusades. Attuned to the symbolic nature of the gesture, the lady fretted each time a petal fell, and faithfully tried to stitch the flower back together. When the rose finally disintegrated, she was left with a beautiful piece of lace, a minute filigree of buttonhole stitches.

Today needle lace is still made by tracing an outline of a flower or leaf on paper and then filling in the design using only a needle and thread. Lace can also be made by a technique that developed in the early 16th century—weaving a pattern with fine threads wound onto bobbins. Since this lace is worked on a pillow, it is called both bobbin lace and pillow lace.

Painstaking to create and enormously expensive to buy, lace was used sparingly in the home until the 19th century and the invention of machine lace. Hence, for 300 years it was primarily a personal adornment for men and women of power and fashion. Initially husbands outdid wives in festooning themselves with extraordinary amounts of lace—4,000 yards for one outfit worn by Henry III of France, for example. But by the 18th century aristocratic women had caught up with their male counterparts, and French lace, for example, became so widely popular that the English kings worried about the balance of trade. Laws were passed forbidding the importing of foreign laces, but smugglers evaded them effortlessly with a variety of ingenious ploys, including baking laces into loaves of bread or swaddling it around babies.

Lace attracted not only smugglers but thieves. Although lace was as valuable as jewels, robbers preferred to purloin lace since it never turned out to be paste. They became so adept at stealing lace that ladies who rode in coaches were advised to sit with their backs to the driver lest a thief slash the coach back and snatch their fontanges and lappets —a towering streamered headdress of lace popular in the early 1700s.

Although lace was beloved by the aristocracy and Catherine de Médicis and Mary Queen of Scots were skilled at lacemaking, it was the poor who primarily labored at its production, a task that might proceed at the rate of an inch a day. Working conditions for lace makers were often grueling. If even *haline grasse* (bad breath) could spoil the color of France's prized silk blond lace, working near a smoky fire was out of the question. Many women spent the winter months laboring in cow barns, relying on bovine warmth to ward off the cold. The threads they used were finer than we can envision; a contemporary sewing thread appears as thick as a rope when placed under a magnifying glass next to the delicate threads used for antique laces—spun from a long-fibered flax that is no longer grown. Today the most exquisite flax thread available is only about one-fifth as fine as the old thread.

The role of lace as a fashionable symbol of wealth and power ended with the advent of two revolutions—one French and the other Industrial. The demise of Marie Antoinette and her flamboyant court at the end of the 18th century made the wearing of lace in France not only inadvisable but dangerous. Across Europe lace tumbled from fashion at the very time when machines began to take over the task of lace making. The village lace maker was on her way to becoming an anachronism.

Machine-made net was first produced in 1764, but it was not until John Heathcoat perfected his loom in 1808 in the south of England that machine-made fabrics began to rival the quality of lace made by hand. When Queen Victoria was married in 1840, she wore handmade English laces in an attempt to promote that dying art, but the quality of English industrial lace was evidenced by her veil of machine net embroidered with handmade floral appliqués.

As the 19th century progressed, mills sprang up in England and elsewhere in Europe, producing yard after yard of lace finery at prices that catered not to the aristocracy but to the middle classes. Fine linens and lace became the hallmark of every well-appointed home. Windows were curtained from floor to ceiling, pillows trimmed with frills, lamps nestled on doilies, and sofas draped with antimacassars. The introduction of the jacquard loom about 1836 permitted the subtle weave of damask to be manufactured in quantity by use of hole-punched pattern cards rather than the memories of professional weavers. Fancy tablecloths and napkins, beautifully edged sheets, pillow shams, and towels, once as expensive as furniture, could be used by all manner of Victorian families.

The new popularity of lace in the home inspired generations of Victorians to try their hands at lace-related techniques. Employing crochet hooks, knitting needles, and tatting shuttles, they produced trimmings and borders, and even bed-size pieces. By the 1950s and '60s, when modernism and streamlined houses were in vogue, these home crafts diminished in popularity, but today they are being revived as an offshoot of the glorious new interest in vintage textiles.

Brought down from attics and rescued from the shelves of antiques shops, linens and lace are experiencing a renaissance. Easy to live with, easy to store, they are practical collectibles. Versatile, beautiful, and imbued with the romance of history, they add softness and elegance to our home furnishings and accessories. Once a rarity, linens and lace are for us the luxuries of everyday life, treasures to be appreciated for the beauty they bring to our world.

THE ROMANCE OF LINENS AND LACE

Although the white purity and quiet romance of linens and lace are now made welcome in homes from country to contemporary, the popular appeal of these soft-spoken textiles has more to do with matters of the soul than with questions of style. Linens and lace please on a deeply personal level—the tranquil light that suffuses a room when a window is dressed in lace, the luxurious feel of fine linen sheets, the celebratory mood created by damask napkins—even when dining alone. Linens and lace were once rarities, but now they are luxuries to be lived with, enjoyed, and used with imagination.

DRESSING

THE

BED

AND BATH

One of the most romantic rooms in the home, the bedroom—the *bedchamber*—has always been a place where linens and lace have been used lavishly. The intricate detail and feminine trims of bed linens and hangings create an inviting and intimate setting that rewards not only the eye but the sense of touch: few things are as tactilely pleasing as fine sheets. Today's all-cotton 200-thread-count percale sheets, available in no-iron finishes, are both a wonderful indulgence and a worthwhile investment. Durable enough to last a lifetime, they have the added benefit of faggoting, embroidery, soft ruffles, eyelet trim, and other details reminiscent of old-fashioned sheets.

Collectors seeking vintage versions will find much to choose from and much that is

A study in wonderful textures: crisp crochet contrasts with the softness of a ruffled linen sheet and a white-on-white Marseilles spread, *above and left*. Its embossed woven flowers and garlands provide a subtle counterpoint to the faded flowers of a Victorian chintz quilt.

still affordable—even when it comes to pure linen sheets and shams, the connoisseur's choice of bed covering. Fine linen has an incomparable feel and only gets softer and whiter with age and washing. The sole drawback to vintage sheets, whether linen or cotton, is their variety of odd sizes; beds and pillows were not standardized until the 20th century. Prior to that time women stitched sheets to suit whatever bedroom furnishings they had. These sheets were, of course, all flat, a design element that enabled thrifty housewives to cut down on laundering by using a sheet twice. On washday, the top sheet would be moved to the bottom so that only a single fresh one need be added. Inventive homemakers also devised a clever means of extending the life of their linens by cutting a worn sheet down the center, reversing the panels so

Against a backdrop of vintage Nottingham lace curtains, a romantic cast-iron bed, *left,* is dressed with a knitted popcorn-stitch spread and scalloped, backless shams laid over European square pillows. *Above,* freshly laundered linens are tied with a ribbon as they would have been in an Edwardian linen closet.

***Overleaf,* fancy embroidery, eyelet, and various kinds of lace create an environment of welcome and comfort.**

A sweep of sheer mosquito netting gives a mahogany-stained rattan bed, made up with a mix of tailored and ruffled shams, a tropical feeling, *far left and below left.* The duvet cover, like the pillows, is detailed with buttons, *below far left,* in the traditional European way. *Left and below,* vintage paisley shawls cover a pair of Jenny Lind beds plumped with square pillows and family linens.

that the center edges were on the outside, and sewing the revived sheet back together for a few more turns.

Vintage pillowcases were also custom-stitched to suit each bedroom, and it was on these that needlewomen lavished their skills, trimming them with everything from crisp tailored edging to soft ruffles, medallions of lace, and elaborate monograms. Shams were sewn for everything from delicate breakfast pillows and neck rolls to large European squares and 6-foot-long Victorian bolsters, the latter of which can be adapted for contemporary use by stuffing them with two or three standard pillows and tying the ends with satin ribbons.

Today's beds, decked in fine linen and plumped with romantic pillows, need only an appropriate spread for a finishing touch. In Victorian times, beds were often dressed with an elaborate cover which would be replaced at night with a simpler one that would stand up to tossing and turning. Such a daytime showpiece might be fashioned from a beautiful lace curtain or a finely detailed damask tablecloth.

Counterpanes that make both excellent day and night covers are white-on-white Marseilles spreads. Produced from the late 19th century onward (many old patterns are still being manufactured today), these spreads have wonderful designs

Canopied with lace and piled with ivory patterned pillows, this gold- and silver-leafed four-poster becomes the most romantic of retreats, *above, right, and far right*. Its damask swagged skirt and lace petticoat are gathered with tasseled silken cords.

woven into the fabric. Other attractive—and equally practical—white-on-white vintage spreads range from white wedding quilts to the crocheted or knitted spreads made in the 1930s and '40s, when women avidly pursued needlework as a hobby.

Beautiful counterpanes such as these, paired with a simple box-pleated dust ruffle or set off with a length of crocheted lace tacked around the edge of the bed, may make such an eloquent statement that no other decorative touches are needed. However, centuries of incurable romantics have devised a variety of ways of filling a bedroom with rich flourishes, from four-posters swathed in draperies and tied with tassels to wooden canopy beds festooned with lacy overhangs, perhaps fashioned

The simple lines of a whitewashed Edwardian bathroom are softened with linen towels decorated with crocheted lace and cutwork, *right*. *Below,* the airy, star-shaped netted doily echoes the graceful scrolls of cast-iron shelf brackets.

from fine filet tablecloths. Simpler versions of this look include curtains hung from rods attached to the ceiling, headboards upholstered with cutwork cloths, and layered eyelet dust ruffles that mimic old-fashioned petticoats.

The Victorian gentlewoman brought the petticoat effect to her bathroom also, rimming the tub with lace. Today, surrounding a sink with a beautiful lace or linen skirt, something that can easily be accomplished with Velcro, is still one of the simplest ways

The rich detailing and delicate patterns of linens inspire proud displays —a collection of hand towels hung from a bentwood rack, *left;* sheets and pillowcases stacked in a linen-upholstered cupboard and tied with grosgrain ribbons, *below;* and hand towels, each with a different lace edging, layered over a white rack, *right.*

to give a bathroom a romantic mood. The shower curtain, backed by a liner, may be a diaphanous lace panel, and towel racks can display a collection of hand towels with beautiful embroidery or tatted edges. Before pile-woven terrycloth was introduced in 1841, bath linens were literally linens (or cottons). With their tactile appeal and beautiful weaves, old-fashioned towels still add a luxurious touch whether hung on a peg rack to await guests, or stacked in a crisp pile atop a chest, which may well be filled with many other treasures of linen and lace.

GRACING
THE
TABLE

Whether it is a summertime tea on the porch or a formal dinner for sixteen, a meal becomes a special one as much because of the way it is presented as because of the food that is served. Traditionally, an essential part of a meal's magical look has been beautiful linens, finery brought out to dress the table in its festive best.

Fine damask cloths have been used on European tables since the Middle Ages when the Crusaders, returning from Damascus, brought back the wondrous, finely wrought fabrics they found there. Beginning in the mid-13th century, the complicated art of damask weaving flourished in the flax-growing countries of France and Flanders. Today the richly woven patterns the Crusaders admired are still being made.

While a beautiful damask or tailored cloth gives a table a quiet elegance, lace

A drawnwork cloth, edged with morning glories, adds a fanciful air to a summer tea by the sea, *above*. The ivy pattern of the tea cozy, *left,* shows off the talents of an expert crocheter.

creates a different mood of charm and grace. A particularly effective way to display lace cloths—one that allows the collector to display several prized possessions at once —is to layer two or three on a single table, creating an interesting play of light and shadow. Another way to highlight the delicate work on a lace cloth is to pair it with a chintz or soft pastel underskirt.

If the finish of a table is especially magnificent, it may need only a touch of lace —tray cloths or lace mats, perhaps each with a different kind of work—at each place, with doilies as coasters. Handsome substitutes for mats are dresser scarves and lace runners, which can give each side of a wood table a sweep of lace.

For a summer lunch in the garden, a 1930s kitchen tablecloth, decorated with rambling roses, sets an appropriately floral note echoed by chintz floral pillows. Lacy touches include an embroidered cutwork napkin, *above far left,* and a star-pointed crochet-trimmed basket liner, *above left.*

Sometimes a square cloth is the best choice for a round table, especially in an outdoor setting like this one, *right,* where sunlight dappled by apple blossoms enhances the lacy patterns of the dangling corners of the cloth. Embroidered scallop-edged white napkins, green majolica plates, an old-fashioned sugar shaker, and bouquets of apple blossoms welcome guests at the garden table, *below and far right.*

Napkins, vintage and new, come in a wide variety of sizes, from diminutive tea and cocktail napkins that might almost be mistaken for delicate handkerchiefs to grand dinner ones meant to cover a portly gentleman's waistcoat from double chin to knees. The numbers carefully embroidered on the corners of some vintage napkins enabled the housekeeper to rotate her linens, ensuring that they received equal wear. And the family monogram—an emblem of pride that also helped identify a household's linen when it was sent out to be laundered—now gives napkins a sense of a personalized past, even when the initials do not match one's own. Beautiful hand towels, plentiful at flea markets and typically embroidered with butterflies and baskets of flowers or edged with crochet, can also be used at the table. Any pretty fabric— perhaps chintz or a beautiful but damaged damask cloth—can be transformed into

Left and below, a woven Marseilles bedspread, edged with sturdy crochet, is a handsome and practical covering for a kitchen table. Shirred white muslin panels, *right,* soften an old-fashioned window and let in light.

Overleaf: An embroidered cutwork napkin is laid beside a creamware basket-weave platter filled with ivorine flatware.

napkins and edged with vintage lace.

In the Victorian heyday of the elaborately dressed table, napkins were folded or rolled and placed in rings. Each member of the family had his or her own ring, engraved with the appropriate initials, so that the napkin could be retrieved at the next meal without having to be washed each time. Rings, which were even made

with sporting motifs and tiny bud vases,

can be collected at antiques shops and

markets, but they also may be replaced

by inventive personal touches—satin rib-

bons or tiny twig wreaths, for example.

Or the end of a napkin can be knotted

and a pink rose, a nosegay of wildflowers,

or even a sachet can be tucked in for

adornment.

With flowers from the meadow, crystal wineglasses, and a light cotton cut- and drawnwork tablecloth, *left and far left,* a simple spring picnic takes on a splendid sense of occasion.

Many other beautiful types of table linens can be found in antiques shops—liners to protect the polish of mahogany trays at tea; basket liners that present dinner rolls in high style (and coincidentally keep them warm); graduated doilies for cake stands; and cozies for sheltering the teapot. Custom-made in the 19th century for the family's special teapots, each prettily decorated cloth is unique; each adds an element of refinement and grace to the table.

Beneath a ruffled organdy balloon shade, a 1930s trolley, *below,* is set for afternoon tea with a Staffordshire transfer-printed service. The deep mahogany wood is the perfect counterpoint for a fine machine-made Honiton-style English lace cloth. *Left,* a silver spoon embossed with fruit is for sprinkling sugar on berries.

A quiet afternoon spent poring over garden catalogues becomes a private celebration when a table is covered with a crisp blue-striped cloth, *left,* and tea-for-one is served on a wicker tray lined with blue linen tray cloth and napkin, *below.*

A
GLIMPSE
AT THE
WINDOW

Lace peacocks offer a proud wel-come, *right. Below,* a lace-edged ta-blecloth, hung as an overscale valance, embellishes simple sheers. Gathered over rods at the center, net floral curtains add a dramatic flourish to a sunny window, *bottom.*

By its very na-ture—an imitation of the tracery of snowflakes or the tapestry of a flower

garden—lace has an enormous affinity for light. Morning sun filtered through a pat-

terned curtain offers an incentive for starting the day. Late afternoon light, gilded by a

sunset, casts delicate shadows across a bleached wood floor. These pleasures are

wonderfully simple to obtain. Although period curtains are scarce—they were usually

worn out in their lifetime due to repeated laundering and exposure to light—their

romantic effect may be re-created with other vintage linens. Lacy tablecloths, clipped

A peek at English cottages shows all manner of lace curtains—shirred on two rods, *left;* arched in a ruffled curve, *below left;* and gracefully parted, *below right.*

at one end with brass rings, have a charming new life at the window. Dresser scarves, the top borders of sheets, and lace-edged towels may be recruited as valances. Windows can also be gracefully framed by swagging a piece of lace around a thick rod, and crisp white curtains can be drawn back with bits of crocheted trim or edged with a lace flounce.

In the seaside village of Porlock, England, the lace with dancing ladies, *left,* in the cottage windows across from the church, is a highlight known to lace enthusiasts. *Below left,* a café curtain affords privacy in a treetop bedroom. Tassels provide jaunty fringe for a lace panel, *below right.*

In addition to vintage fabrics and trims, there are a multitude of new window laces, many of them reproductions of old designs, that have been ardently researched and carefully revived by a number of mills, especially those that still flourish around Nottingham, England. Examples of these laces—as well as the Victorian originals—hang at

the windows of countless stone and whitewashed cottages in England, especially in Devon and the south, where lacemaking blossomed for centuries, and where a wealth of specialty antiques stores makes lace collecting almost irresistible. The ways of displaying lace in this part of England are as limitless as the kinds of lace—fanciful peacocks facing each other at attention, garlands of roses bordered by a curving hem of ruffles, geometric marriages of gauze and openwork.

A glimpse of lace at the window, whether in our own homes or one that captivates us along a country road, links indoors to outdoors and hints to passersby of the warmth of the home within.

Whether a cottage has a thatched bay window or gothic framing and a window box full of flowers, lacy curtains make its panes that much more intriguing—a see-through glimpse that piques the imagination.

A plain window, *far left,* takes on an element of grandeur with a striking Art Nouveau panel of stylized flowers blooming above a white fence.

Little gables, bay windows, and dormers with storybook trim, *above,* seem to lend themselves to lace. One can easily imagine sitting on a window banquette and, between sips from a cup of tea, peeking through the lace motifs to watch the world go by.

In a sun-dappled window, lacy linens become a focal point. *Above left,* the bottom half of a kitchen window is layered with a café curtain and valance on two spring rods. A tray cloth, *above right,* and net panel, *far right,* have such interesting detail that they need only a simple rod. *Below,* eyelet shirred on a ribbon adds a flourish to a pretty collection of china.

A
TOUCH
OF
LACE

**A padded white hanger with lace ap-
pliqué, *below;* and an eyelet-slipcov-
ered one, perfect for a special dress,
right, are two charming uses for odd
bits of lace.**

F or the Victorians
scarcely an object existed, no matter how
humble or functional, that could not be
enhanced by adornment. Decorating today is a more discerning affair, a matter of
selecting the right detail, bestowing the right touch to a room, so that there is a perfect
interplay of pattern and texture, the right blend of spareness and charm.

Linens and lace are wonderful finishing touches. When a piece is singled out as a
decorative accessory, the intricacy of its design and the attention its maker gave to
detail can be appreciated, whether it is the deep tailored hem and monogram on a
tray cloth or the fanciful rose and ivy patterns on a framed handkerchief.

Versatile and fascinating examples of the lace maker's artistry are doilies, plentiful
in attic trunks and in bargain baskets at flea markets and shops. Generations of women
kept their hands from idleness and embellished their homes by crocheting, tatting, and

Above, a collection of lace doilies, some knitted, some crocheted, sit atop white pitchers, a display reminiscent of the classic English jug covers, which are usually weighted with small beads or shells. A crocheted length of lace, *right,* on a simple mantel provides a romantic setting for a still life display. A sheer Ayrshire embroidered tea cloth, *above right,* turned on the diagonal so that the light shows off its delicate patterns, replaces a dresser scarf.

A collection of everyday china and glassware is beautifully framed by lace trim, each with a different motif, *right*. Lace can also be used to line a single shelf, as illustrated by the delicate embroidered net, *far right*.

netting these diminutive circles of lace named for Doyley, an 18th-century London draper. Originally made with the goal of protecting the fine polish of tables from vases, lamps, and potted plants, doilies are now being resurrected after decades of unfashionableness. They are being used to give rooms a light, fresh touch as stylish coasters for wineglasses and teacups as well as pretty antimacassars to drape over a chair back.

One charming variation of the doily—the jug cover—shows the practical aspect of crocheted lace. Weighted down with beads around the edges, these embellished doilies originally protected milk from marauding flies in the pantry. A particularly popular English home craft, these covers were also recruited to shield pitchers of lemonade and milk jugs for tea, as can be surmised by little three-dimensional cro-

cheted teacups found atop some of these bead-edged doilies.

Doilies and other odd bits of linen and lace can be used in countless ways—to decorate a glass-fronted cabinet, line an old wicker sewing basket, or cover a pincushion or coat hanger. Decorative scraps, filled with lavender or potpourri, make wonderful sachets to tuck in a linen closet or to give as gifts. Lace-edged tray cloths, angled on a shelf so that a corner dips invitingly over the edge, can serve as the base for a still life of white pitchers or a favorite collection of glass.

Other larger, miscellaneous linens—huge 19th-century European pillow shams, for example—can be used as attractive

With an eyelet sachet tucked beneath a taffeta bow, a bundle of starched lace-edged huck towels, *above,* is a perfect wedding gift. Even in the smallest foyer a diminutive lace-skirted table offers a wonderful welcome, as well as a handy spot for gardeners to display the morning's pickings, *far left.*

draping for small round tables or bed-

room vanities. Large table napkins may

double as inventive seat covers for side

chairs, with corners tied at each leg. (For

a more elegant look, add tassels or pretty

ribbons.) Napkins with an interesting

weave can play a role as upholstery for a

small chair seat. Sewn together, a pair of

napkins can be a lingerie bag to hang at

the foot of the bed or the back of a door.

Odd bits of linen or lace can be used as

liners for drawers of silverware or other

treasures—a charming way to enhance a

collection.

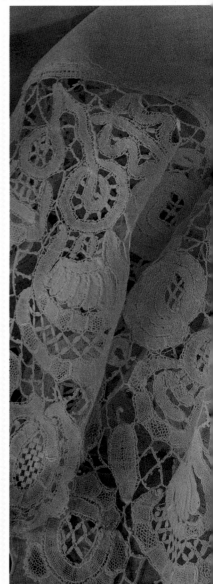

A simple loveseat, *left,* acquires an appealing new look with an ivory linen slipcover, embellished with a lace panel draped over the back. A tea table is set with an eyelet cloth and a napkin edged with Honiton lace roses and thistles, *above.*

Beautiful linens can be showcased on the backs and arms of chairs, *above,* or used to upholster special pieces of furniture like this delicately carved Victorian side chair, which frames a piece of embroidery as artfully as the handkerchief hanging above it, *right.* A little Victorian pique laundry bag with eyelet trim, perfect for pretty lingerie, hangs by its blue satin ribbon, *far right.*

A COLLECTOR'S GUIDE

As collectors know, the thread of a splendid story is often entwined with the intricate patterns of linen and lace. Among the pillow shams tucked in the corner of a tiny antiques shop, one might come from a young girl's trousseau, the embroidery begun as soon as she could hold a needle in her hand. Another might have been imported from Belgium or Ireland for an elegant society matron and kept pristine by her personal laundress. Still another might seem almost unused, as if it were too precious to sleep on.

Linens and lace were extraordinarily personal items in their day, crafted with care or purchased at great expense, and cherished by their owners. With the exception of trousseau pieces and museum-quality rarities, the age of the object or its style is not really relevant to buying decisions: late Victorian linens are as prized as early ones. Aesthetics should be the collector's primary criterion, followed by condition and quality. This means that one can afford to follow the dictates of one's heart—especially if such passionate impulses are backed up by a generous helping of practical knowledge.

SHOPPING

FOR

VINTAGE

LINENS

Most linen and lace experts seem to have a remarkable inner radar that guides them to just the right purchase. Certainly it stems from steeping themselves in books and museum exhibits, but what separates the dabbler from the maven is a discerning employment of *all* the senses. One New York dealer is fond of talking about listening to the material. "Fold it, crinkle it, *hear* it," she is

The early morning light of London's Bermondsey and Camden Passage flea markets reveals a multitude of treasures, from tea cloths and cozies, *left,* to doilies and shams, *below,* that once adorned proud Victorian homes.

Against a wall covered with a softly gathered embroidered drawnwork cloth, *below,* **London shopkeeper Stephen Lunn displays a handsome range of reproduction pillows. Lace panels and inserts,** *right,* **tempt shoppers in an open-air market.**

Overleaf, **the Mendeses' shop in Brighton, England, is renowned for its wonderful textiles, rugs, and linens.**

always advising: if fabric is dry or brittle, a warning crackle signals that fibers are about to split.

The sense of smell is also important. In addition to the telltale crackle, dryness can also be spotted by the flat dusty smell of lifeless fibers. Another danger sign is the aroma of bleach, a substance that did not enter the laundry until the 1890s. If bleach has not been fully rinsed away the fibers will eventually disintegrate.

Collectors also can educate themselves through their hands. Quality, quite simply, *feels* good. Linen is cool to the touch and stiffer than cotton. Machine-made lace, too, is stiffer than its handmade cousin—not from starch but from an inherent brittleness that never softens, even with washing.

In distinguishing machine from hand work, another sense—sight—will help, especially when aided by a magnifying glass. So important is this little tool that seasoned collectors are seldom seen without it. In general, machine lace has an

In Pirouette, housed in a tiny Tudor building in Exeter, England, a lace runner embellishes a cupboard filled with vintage dresses and bed linens, *far left. Above,* table-cloths, curtains, and lacy spreads hang side by side in a dealer's open-air booth, making it easy for a shopper to imagine creative uses. Beautifully edged vintage pillows, *left,* can be mimicked with lacy trims, *below,* sewn to custom pillows.

overall regularity and stiffness of design. But some early machines were operated by hand, and their laces have the quirky individuality of handwork. Examining the back of the lace with a magnifying glass will help resolve questions. Machines could only work in one direction, hence a leaf would be outlined with two threads and "floaters" (looped threads) would be left when the machine skipped to the next design. By contrast, a lace maker who made her living from precise work would never be so careless as to leave loops, even on the back of her work. A careful examination of threads will also help a collector distinguish machine from handmade lace. Industrial looms used coarser and less expensive threads, whereas lace makers, especially those with talent, had the delicacy of touch to use gossamer threads.

To assess quality, linens—even thick Marseilles spreads—should be held up to the light. In the 19th century, one of the first things young girls learned was the darning stitch. Often these mends are quite charming and add to the appeal of the piece—if the rest of the fabric is sturdy. Ask the dealer for permission to tug at the corners of the mend. If the fibers tend to give, the purchase should be passed up. Holding the fabric up to the light should also help spot thin and worn areas, a sequence of cracks, or a pattern of erosion—additional signs that a fabric will not stand up to wear.

Unlike linens, mends in lace are usually inconspicuous. Ask the dealer if the piece has ever been mended, or else washing may provide a surprise or two. A New Orleans textile conservator restored the whiteness of a wonderful but terribly yellowed mid-19th-century altar cloth—only to discover mends done with colored thread, chosen to match the once-yellowed hue of the lace.

Most of the vintage linens and lace encountered today date from the Victorian era to the 1930s, but it is possible to chance upon a rare find tucked in a bag with scraps. It is just such serendipity that keeps collectors searching.

At favorite shops like **Brocante** in Cheltenham, England, where curbside trunks and blanket stands are laden with linens, it is always wise to travel with a tape measure in hand. Beautifully trimmed vintage pillow shams, sheets, and spreads come in a wide range of sizes. Prior to the 20th century when beds and pillows were standardized, linens were usually custom sewn and embellished to suit the particular beds of the house.

CARE
AND
LAUNDERING

Black lace and net should be dipped in ale and ironed out between sheets of paper, and wound on cards until required," advised the *Young Englishwoman* in 1872. Over the years, the prescriptions for care and cleaning of linen and lace have been as wide-ranging as the materials themselves. Today, some experts still debate whether it is safe to put linens in the sun (the rain-bound English defer on the sunlight question), but on the whole, collectors concur on the treatments explained below.

Sometimes these techniques are learned through trial and error. Most dealers advise never washing old, fine lace so as to steer clear of the risk of ruining a work of art that took hundreds and hundreds of hours to make. Fine lace should be handled only by a professional. Names of experts may be found at your local historical society or museum. However, most Victorian and machine-made lace that adorns the average pillowcase or tablecloth can withstand gentle washing.

Hand-washing with a mild soap such as Ivory Liquid or Orvus is the treatment advised for most linens used in the home. For table linens, when the inevitable spill does occur, run boiling water through the stain as soon as possible. Stretch the napkin or tablecloth over a bucket and pour hot water right from the teakettle. Then toss the whole cloth in the bucket and let it soak in mild, pure soap. The key is not to let the stain set. When faced with a lingering spot, soak it in a solution of one part water and one part lemon juice with a pinch of salt. If the stain proves stubborn, immerse it in a bath of nonchlorine bleach and set in direct sunlight. Soak several days if necessary, changing the solution daily.

When linens yellow, the time-honored whitening method is to lay them on a still-dewy lawn to dry. In the 17th and 18th centuries, every village had a bleaching field, but some lawns had more magical properties than others. The bleaching fields of Flanders were so renowned that linens from all over Europe would be sent there. The combination of dew, grass, and sun does, in fact, produce a chemical reaction that adds brilliance to linens, but recent research has revealed that, just as sunlight burns fair skin, so does it distress some fibers. Experts therefore advise that all but the sturdiest linens be dried indoors, even if whiteness has to be sacrificed.

When cleaning heirloom linens that need especially sensitive care, it is important to clean them without rubbing or agitation. The motion of the water should be the only active agent. Begin by removing covered buttons or hooks and placing them in labeled envelopes so that they can be stitched back on correctly. Next, line the sink with an old towel that can be used as a sling for lifting the wet textile. Mix four tablespoons of Ivory Liquid or one tablespoon Orvus WA paste with a gallon of warm water. (Use the same ratio for larger amounts.) Immerse the piece in the solution, but do not pour water directly on the textile or rub the fibers. After 45 minutes of soaking, drain the water while running the tap into the basin at the same time—a gentle, indirect rinsing process that causes no stress to the fabric. (Textiles are most fragile when they are weighted with water.) Rinse for about 45 minutes or until all traces of soap have vanished. Then cradle the textile in the towel, gently press off any excess water, and using the towel, raise the textile out of the sink and place onto a dry towel. Keeping the textile in its sling, blot carefully, using as many additional dry towels as you need. When the textile is more damp than wet, spread it on a Formica, glass, or other nonwooden surface and gently reshape it with your hands. If the shape is difficult to hold, or if there is a scalloped lace trim, anchor the edges with clean kitchen glasses or jelly jars positioned so they extend just a quarter inch onto the fabric. Such proper blocking may eliminate the need for ironing.

When linens are still damp, it is time to think about ironing. If ironing must be postponed, roll up damp linens and put them in a plastic bag in the refrigerator. When it is time for ironing, shake the linens out gently and hang them over a rack until almost dry. Cover the iron with a Teflon guard (one size fits all) to avoid spurts of steam and staining. Work on the back side of the fabric whenever possible to preserve the raised stitching of embroidery and lace and keep the fabric free of shiny spots. Pressing with the grain will keep the fabric's shape. Flatten—don't pull—the cloth if it has lace inserts. When ironing a large vintage tablecloth, first lay a sheet on the floor under your board so that it stays clean.

If extra body is needed, try a spray sizing product rather than a starch. Before putting linens away for long-term storage, wash out sizing and starch in soft water (hard water leaves a residue of iron which over time rusts and leaves brown spots).

When vintage linens are not in use, they should be wrapped in acid-free paper and stored in a closet, an acid-free box, or a cardboard, metal, or wooden box lined with unbleached muslin. A safeguard against both aging and yellowing, acid-free paper is available at drugstores, stationery stores, and some hardware stores. Long table runners or cloths that will retain fold lines should be rolled in acid-free tubes or cardboard tubes that have been wrapped first with acid-free paper. It is best not to add potpourri or lavender sachets to your storage box because the oil from these dried flowers can eat away at fine fabrics. However, linens that are used and aired regularly, may be freely scented.

A LACE GLOSSARY

AYRSHIRE, named after a county in Scotland, is a delicate white-on-white embroidery, usually executed on muslin or fine cambric lawn. Often it has openwork detailing.

BATTENBERG LACE took its place in decorative arts history as a description of a certain kind of lace made with lacy strips or tapes sewn into an intricate pattern when Queen Victoria's daughter and granddaughter both married into the German Battenberg family. These tapes were so simple to make that they became one of the first lace products of the Industrial Revolution. Often Battenberg lace is elaborately ornamented with handwork.

CROCHETED LACE, linked rows of chain stitches accomplished with a hook, is what helped rescue Ireland from the potato famine in the 1840s. The basic techniques were introduced there with the hope of alleviating the plight of the poor, and workers took the art to such heights that Irish crochet soon produced very passable imitations of 17th-century Venetian raised points as well as elegant collars, shawls, and other lacy goods. One of the most glorious hallmarks of Irish crochet has been a three-dimensional rose made with tiny concentric circles of raised petals.

CUTWORK, a lacy fabric related to eyelet, *below,* but more elaborate, is created by cutting away threads of a woven fabric to create an intricate pattern of open spaces. It is often elaborately decorated with white embroidery. Cutwork found on museum laces is usually much finer than that made today and is more closely related to drawnwork.

DRAWNWORK is the needlewoman's refinement of the weaver's art. Though it is worked with the warp and weft of a cloth, the fabric is essentially re-created. Some threads are removed and others looped together with embroidered stitches, until the finished piece has a beautiful open pattern.

EYELET is made by surrounding delicate holes, which usually have an oval, circular, or teardrop shape, with small running stitches—just as an eye is rimmed with lashes. Strictly speaking, eyelet is closer to embroidery than to lace making, a fact reflected by its commonly used French name, **BRODERIE ANGLAISE.**

FILET LACE was a favorite pastime of Catherine de Médicis, to whom a number of 16th-century Italian lace pattern books are dedicated. This gridlike lace is made by embellishing a hand-knitted square net with darned detail or by working crocheted stitches in geometric patterns.

KNITTED LACE, sometimes called Viennese lace, relies on the same techniques used to make mittens and sweaters. However, the thread is far finer, the needles thinner, and the pattern very airy and open.

KNOTTED LACE is very similar to its netted cousin, below. However, its knots, which both sailors and macramé enthusiasts will recognize, are made solely with a sewing needle.

NETTED LACE, made by knotting thread wound around a shuttle or netting needle, invokes the techniques used to make fishing nets and to craft the mesh canopy bed hangings popular in colonial America. The secret to the art of netting is that one end of the thread is tied to a doorknob or heavy object so that tension can be maintained as each knot is tied.

TATTING, called *frivolité* in France, relies on a shuttle to make loops of thread, usually in circles, which are linked to form a design.

The beauty of linens is often in the details: *above*, white-on-white embroidery with motifs ranging from delicate sprigs to boldly outlined flowers reminiscent of crewel work. At *left*, napkins decorated with cheerful embroidered daisies and drawnwork hems. *Below left*, at antiques shops, tables like this with inviting piles of crocheted lace and embroidered linens immediately draw collectors. *Below*, a new machine-made curtain panel evokes designs popular in Victorian times.

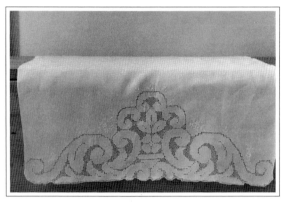

The lacemaker's talent is illustrated by this fine hand-made panel, *above left,* with mythological figures set against a spiderweb of threads. The panel is bordered with scalloped net and embellished with carefully stitched flowers. *Left,* a simple linen hand towel takes on a new elegance with a cutwork hem executed in a classical scroll pattern. *Below,* a gracefully scalloped tea tablecloth shows the beauty of filet work—clusters of flowers whose petals and leaves are executed on a geometric grid.

Today, many new linens are ably capturing the detail and richness of those from the Victorian period. These pillow shams, *right,* shown at Stephen Lunn's London shop, include Battenberg tape motifs, embroidery, and eyelet decoration.

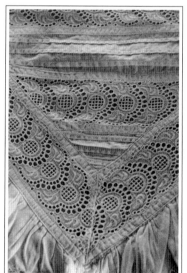

Near right, a tablecloth catches the light in a shop window, just one of the many displays that show off the fine work in vintage linens. *Far right,* a machine-made Nottingham lace curtain panel with a flower-filled urn in the center cartouche. *Above left,* a gathering of vintage pieces with Battenberg lace and intricate detailing. *Above right,* a broderie anglaise–pillow sham detailed with alternating layers of tucked cotton with a ruffled trim.

MONOGRAMS Heraldry and housekeeping—it is from these two traditions that come the monograms that decorate the damask tablecloths, counterpanes, and bath towels we display in our homes. In the 17th and 18th centuries linens and indeed all fabrics were extraordinarily expensive. So just as we now put iron-on tags on our children's camp clothes, women cross-stitched little initials, often in red, so that the household linens could be retrieved when sent to the local laundry. But such pragmatism should not obscure the fact that the monogram, no matter how simply sewn, was always a mark of pride, a visible sign that a family had achieved elegant trappings, from petticoats to pillow cases.

Girls from all walks of life labored at cross-stitch alphabet samplers from the moment their hands could hold a needle. Some, too, practiced another sort of sampler where name after name was satin-stitched in beautiful script. Such proud hallmarks are actually not difficult to execute at home today, especially if you have a sewing machine with an embroidery attachment. And while the work may appear tedious at first, you will quickly learn the skills that made the monograms of long ago.

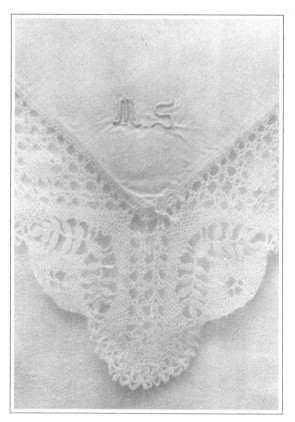

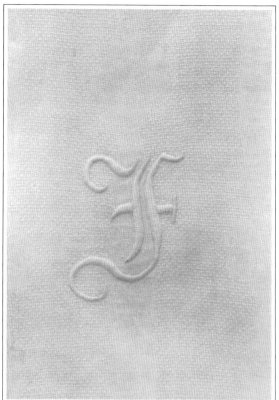

Left, a damask hand towel is personalized with an inventive monogram shaped by embroidered forget-me-nots. Above, fine lawn handkerchiefs like these always sported monograms so that they would make their way back to their owners after washing. Above right, a Gothic-style hallmark. Right, a single initial on a linen tray cloth symbolizes a family's pride in its home.

RESOURCES

C   Conservation
MU Museum
T   To the trade
M   Manufacturer
O   Organization
S   School
MO Mail order
R   Retailer

R E T A I L E R S

Amazing Lace and Linen **R,MO**
P.O. Box 5406
Richmond, CA 94805-5406

Anderson Gallery **R**
21 Davis Street
Keene, NH 03431
(603) 352-7855

Ann Lawrence **R**
250 West 39th Street
New York, NY 10018
(212) 302-6659

And Old Lace **R**
320 Court Street
Salem, OR 97301
(503) 585-6010

Boutique de France **R**
735A Middleneck Road
Great Neck, NY 11024
(516) 466-6074

Cherchez **R**
862 Lexington Avenue
New York, NY 10021
(212) 737-8215

Collector Antiques **R**
3123 Magazine Street
New Orleans, LA 70115
(504) 897-0904

E. Braun & Co. **C,R**
717 Madison Avenue
New York, NY 10021
(212) 838-0650

Eileen Russell **R**
439 Ridgedale Drive North
Worthington, OH 43085
(614) 885-7968

Elaine Wilmarth **R**
5715 Sir Galahad Road
Glenn Dale, Maryland 20769
(301) 464-1567
By appointment

The Fabric of Society **R**
2120 California Street, #14
San Francisco, CA 94115
(415) 929-8519
By appointment

Filigree Linens and Lace **R**
1210 Yonge Street
Toronto, ON M4T 1W1
Canada
(416) 961-5223

Forget-Me-Nots **R**
P.O. Box 7318
Carmel, CA 93921
(408) 624-9080

Françoise Nunnallé **R**
105 West 55th Street
New York, NY 10019
(212) 246-4281
By appointment

Grandma's Trousseau Antique
Linens **R**
110 East Andrews Drive
Atlanta, GA 30305
(404) 233-7388

Howard Kaplan's French Country
Store **R**
35 East 10th Street
New York, NY 10003
(212) 674-1000

Jabberwocky **R**
Cheri B. Carter
310 East Main Street
Fredericksburg, TX 78624

Jean Hoffman/Jana Starr **R**
236 East 80th Street
New York, NY 10028
(212) 535-6930

Katy Kane Inc. **R**
34 West Ferry Street
New Hope, PA 18938
(215) 862-5873

The Lace Broker **R**
252 Newbury Street
Boston, MA 02116
(617) 267-5954

Lace Cottage **R**
88 Lexington Avenue, Suite 12C
New York, NY 10016
(212) 689-1268

Laci's
2982 Adeline Street
Berkeley, CA 94703
(415) 843-7178

Laura Fisher **R**
Antique Quilts and Americana
1050 Second Avenue
New York, NY 10022
(212) 838-2596

Leslie Batchelor Designs **R**
123 North Cushing
Olympia, WA 98502
(206) 357-7703

Linens and Lace, Ltd. **R**
1015 Princess Street
Alexandria, VA 22314
(703) 549-5148

Notable Accents and Tokens of the
Past **R**
6701 Snider Place
Dallas, TX 75205
(214) 349-5525

Promesse **R**
88 Lexington Avenue, #12C
New York, NY 10016
(212) 689-1268

Rue de France **R,MO**
78 Thames Street
Department PB 587
Newport, RI 02840
(401) 846-2084

Simply Lace **R**
231 Wall Street
Huntington, NY 11743
(516) 549-0105

Sue Fisher King **R**
3067 Sacramento Street
San Francisco, CA 94115
(415) 922-2276

Sussex Antiques **R**
P.O. Box 7964
Bedford, NY 10506
(914) 241-2919

Treasures With a Past **R**
21 Davis Street
Keene, NH 03431
(603) 352-7855

Trouvaille Française **R**
New York City
(212) 737-6015
By appointment only

Victoria Falls **R**
451 West Broadway
New York, NY 10012
(212) 254-2433

Victorian Garden **R**
136-58 72nd Avenue
Flushing, NY 11367
(718) 544-1657

Victoria's Lace Design **R,MO**
P.O. Box 583
Oakville, ON L6J 5B4
Canada
(416) 847-0838

The Wicker Garden **R**
1318 Madison Avenue
New York, NY 10128
(212) 348-1166

Worldly Goods **R**
52 Purchase Street
Rye, NY 10580
(914) 967-1770

Woven Waters **R**
St. Peters Village
St. Peters, PA 19470
(215) 687-0708

MANUFACTURERS

Anichini Linea Casa **M**
150 Fifth Avenue, Room 524
New York, NY 10011
(212) 982-7274

Au Lit **M**
642 Rue de Courcelle, #404
Montreal, QB H4C 3C5
Canada
(514) 933-5070

Brook Hill Linens Inc. **M**
698 Madison Avenue
New York, NY 10021
(212) 688-1113

Jane Wilmer **M**
Washington, DC
(202) 966-1484

Katha Diddel Home Collection for
Twin Panda **M**
420 Madison Avenue, Suite 804
New York, NY 10017
(212) 751-2850

Le Jacquard Français **M**
200 Lovers Lane
Culpeper, VA 22701
(701) 825-0770

Paperwhite Ltd. **M**
P.O. Box 956
Fairfax, CA 94930
(415) 457-7673

The Quaker Lace Company **T,M**
24 West 40th Street
New York, NY 10018
(212) 221-0480

A Touch of Ivy **M,R**
193 Prince Street
New York, NY 10013
(212) 334-0371

The Ulster Weaving Co, Ltd. **M,I**
148 Madison Avenue
New York, NY 10016
(212) 684-5534

MAIL ORDER

Amazing Lace and Linen **R,MO**
P.O. Box 5406
Richmond, CA 94805-5406

Claesson Co. **MO**
P.O. Box Box 130
Cape Neddick, ME 03902
(207) 363-5059

Claudia Graham
Designs in Crochet
40 Seaview Terrace
Unit 40
Guilford, CT 06437
(203) 453-5118

Faith's Lacery **MO**
702 North State Street
South Elgin, IL 60123
(312) 635-3080

Lace Country **MO**
21 West 38th Street, 16th floor
New York, NY 10018

Lace Merchant **MO**
P.O. Box 222
Planeville, MI 49080

Linen and Lace **MO**
Dept. V8
4 Lafayette Street
Washington, MO 63090
(800) 332-LACE

P. Pillow Co. **MO**
P.O. Box 5705
Akron, OH 44372
(216) 666-1958

Scandia Down Store **MO**
P.O. Box 88819
Seattle, WA 98188
(206) 251-5050

Victoria's Lace Design **R,MO**
P.O. Box 583
Oakville, ON L6J 5B4
Canada
(416) 847-0838

MUSEUMS IN THE
U.S.A.

Brooklyn Museum **MU**
Costume and Textile Department
200 Eastern Parkway
Brooklyn, NY 11238
(718) 638-5000
By appointment

Cooper-Hewitt Museum **MU**
Fifth Avenue at 91st Street
New York, NY 10128
(212) 860-6868

Flagler Museum **MU**
P.O. Box 969
Coconut Row
Palm Beach, FL 33480
(407) 655-2833

Historic Deerfield **MU**
Box 321
Deerfield, MA 01342
(413) 774-5581

MUSEUMS, SHOPS, AND MARKETS IN ENGLAND

Alfie's Antique Market **R**
Audrey Fields
1325 Church Street/
Edgeware Road
London NW 8

Antiquarius **R**
135 Kings Road
London SW3

Beer Lace Shop **R**
2 The Cross
Beer, Devon
02-972-1729

Joachim and Betty Mendes **R**
Decorative Antiques & Textiles
66 Upper North Street
Brighton BN13FL East Sussex
02-737-75978

Brocante
197 London Road
Charlton Kings
Cheltenham, Glos GL50 INN
02-422-2243120

Castle Antiques **R**
Eileen Marsh
34 High Street
Arundel, Sussex
09-275-2927

Cocoa **R**
7 Queens Circus
Montpelier
Cheltenham
Glos GL50 1S4
02-422-233588

Fine Linens **R**
Axholme
Lovercoat Lane
Needingworth, Huntingdon
Cambs PE17 3TU
04-803-01773

Gallery of Antique Costumes and
Textiles **MU**
2 Church Street
London NW8

Lacis **R**
High Street
Budleigh Salterton

Luton Museum and Art Gallery
MU
Wardown Park
Luton, LU2 7HA

Min Lundie **R**
47 South Row, Covent Garden
London
01-435-3108

Museum of Costume and Lace **MU**
Rougemont House, Castle Street
Exeter
03-922-65858

Paul Jones **R**
183 Kings Road
London SW3

Stephen Lunn **R,MO**
86 New Kings Road
Parsons Green
London SW6
01-736-4638

Victoria and Albert Museum **MU**
Cromwell Road
South Kensington SW7 2RL
01-938-8500

Pirouette
5 West Street
Exeter
03-924-32643

Wyn Gilette **R**
34 Upper North Street
Brighton BN13FG
27-372-1415

Zebra Antique Linens **R**
58 Mill Lane
West Hampstead NW6
01-435-3108

MUSEUMS IN OTHER EUROPEAN COUNTRIES

Atelier de la Dentelle de Bayeux
MU
6 Rue Lambert Leforestier
14400 Bayeux
France

Atelier de la Reine Mathilde **MU**
2 Rue de la Poissonnerie
14400 Bayeux
France

Kunstindustrimuseet **MU**
Bredgade 68
1260 Copenhagen K
Denmark

Musée de Costumes et de
Dentelles **MU**
Rue de la Violette
B-1000 Bruxelles
Belgium

Musée de la Dentelle du Point
d'Alençon **MU**
33 Rue du Pont-Neuf
6100 Alençon
France

Musée des Arts de la Mode **MU**
108 Rue de Rivoli
75001 Paris
France

Musée des Beaux-Arts et de la
Dentelle **MU**
Rue Charles Aveline
6100 Alençon
France

Museo Poldi Pezzoli **MU**
12 Via Manzoni
Firenze, Italy

Palazzo Davanzati **MU**
Via Porta Rosa
Firenze, Italy

Rijksmuseum **MU**
Stadhouderskade 42
1071 ZD Amsterdam
Holland
020-732121

Textilmuseum **MU**
Vadianstrasse 2
9000 St. Gallen
Switzerland
071-221744

ORGANIZATIONS

Embroidery Council of America **O**
500 Fifth Avenue
New York, NY 10020
(212) 730-0685

International Linen Council **O**
200 Lexington Avenue
New York, NY 10016
(212) 685-0424

International Old Lacers, Inc. **O**
Judy Green Davis
P.O. Box 16186
Phoenix, AZ 85011

Lace Guild of New York **O**
Box 1249, Gracie Station
New York, NY 10028

Lost Art Lacers of North Jersey **O**
RRI Box 114B
Andover, NJ 07821

The National Needlework
Association **O**
230 Fifth Avenue
New York, NY 10010
(212) 685-1646

Union des Arts Decoratif **O**
107, Rue de Rivoli
75001 Paris
France

SCHOOLS

Elizabeth Kurella, Lecturer **S**
P.O. Box 222
Plainwell, MI 49080
(616) 685-9792

International Old Lacers Inc. **S**
Judy Green Davis
P.O. Box 16186
Phoenix, AZ 85011

Scuola de Merietti di Burano **S**
Piazza Galuppi, Isola di Torcello
Venezia, Italy

Thousand Island Craft School **S**
314 John Street
Clayton, NY 13624
Lace making classes

Van Sciver Bobbin Lace **S**
130 Cascadilla Park
Ithaca, NY 14850
(607) 277-0498

TO THE TRADE

Cameo **T**
261 Fifth Avenue
New York, NY 10020
(212) 679-3040

Kirk-Brummel Associates **T**
979 Third Avenue
New York, NY 10022
(212) 477-8590

Lee Jofa **T**
979 Third Avenue
New York, NY 10022
(212) 688-0444

The Quaker Lace Co. **T**
24 West 40th Street
New York, NY 10018
(212) 221-0480

Schumacher **T**
79 Madison Avenue
New York, NY 10016
(212) 213-7909

Waverly Fabrics **T**
79 Madison Avenue
New York, NY 10016
(212) 213-8100

CONSERVATION

Bryce Reveley Gentle Arts **C**
Complete Antique Textile Service
P.O. Box 15832
New Orleans, LA 70115
(504) 895-5628
Cleaning, restoration, conservation,
and appraising. Specializing in lace,
linens, christening and wedding
dresses, samplers, quilts, tapestries,
silk embroidery.

E. Braun and Co. **C**
717 Madison Avenue
New York, NY 10021
(212) 838-0650

Manaufacture Belge de Dentelles
C,R
Galerie de la Reine 6-8
Galerie Royale St. Hubert
B-1000 Bruxelles
Belgium

BIBLIOGRAPHY

Earnshaw, Pat. *The Identification of Lace.* Merlins Bridge, England: Shire Publications Ltd., 1980

Horn, Richard. "The Allure of Lace." *House Beautiful's Home Decorating,* fall 1983, pp. 44–47.

Jones, Julia, and Barbara Deer. *A Calendar of Feasts: Cattern Cakes and Lace.* London: Dorling Kindersley, 1987.

Kraatz, Anne. *Lace: History and Fashion.* New York: Rizzoli, 1989.

Levey, Santina M. *Lace: A History.* London: Victoria and Albert Museum, 1983.

Loveman, Aurelia. *Lace.* Baltimore: The Walters Art Gallery, 1988.

Niles, Bo. *Living with Lace.* New York: Stewart, Tabori, and Chang, 1990.

Palliser, Mrs. Bury. *History of Lace.* New York: Dover, 1984.

Reigate, Emily. *An Illustrated Guide to Lace.* Woodbridge, England: The Antique Collector's Club, 1986.

Staniland, Kay, and Santina M. Levey. *Queen Victoria's Wedding Dress and Lace.* Leeds, England: W. S. Maney & Sons Ltd., 1983.

Wardle, Patricia. *Victorian Lace.* Carlton, England: Ruth Bean, 1982.

Warnick, Kathleen, and Shirley Nilsson. *Legacy of Lace: Identifying, Collecting, and Preserving American Lace.* New York: Crown Publishers, 1988.

Wright, Thomas. *The Romance of the Lace Pillow.* Carlton, England: Ruth Bean, 1982.